On the Preacher and Preaching

ON THE PREACHER
AND PREACHING

by

St. Francis de Sales

Translated, with an Introduction and Notes

by

John K. Ryan

HENRY REGNERY COMPANY
1964

Nihil obstat:

    REVEREND ROBERT P. MOHAN, S.S.

    Censor Deputatus

Imprimatur:

    PATRICK A. O'BOYLE

    Archbishop of Washington

August 10, 1963

PREFACE

THE work that is here called St. Francis de Sales' *On the Preacher and Preaching* is a translation of a letter containing an extended treatment of the subject, written by him on October 5, 1604, and published in 1626 in the first collection of his letters. The text used is that in the critical edition of St. Francis de Sales' works, published at Annecy, 1892-1932, in twenty-six volumes, the first 12 of which were edited by Dom Henry Benedict Mackey, O.S.B. I have been unable to find a previous translation of the letter into English. I have translated literally and have not thought of refining a work that was written without any effort at refinement of style beyond that which St. Francis de Sales necessarily gave to whatever he wrote.

Dom Mackey's scriptural and other bibliographical references have been very helpful, but I have expanded many of his notes and added much new material. In the letter some scriptural texts are in French and others are in Latin; in the translation, the Latin quotations are retained in the text and a translation of them is given in the footnotes. This holds also for certain nonscriptural quotations in Latin. The Confraternity of Christian Doctrine version of the Bible has been used wherever possible, but I have always translated the text as given by St. Francis de Sales. For patristic references J.-P. Migne's *Patrologia latina* and *Patrologia graeca* have been used under the abbreviations P.L. and P.G. Certain subheadings not found in the original letter have been introduced into the text and are printed in large type.

John K. Ryan

School of Philosophy,
The Catholic University of America,
Washington, D. C.,
August 1, 1963

CONTENTS

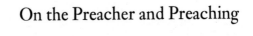

On the Preacher and Preaching

INTRODUCTION

Dᴜʀɪɴɢ his life as a priest and bishop, St. Francis de Sales preached continually, never neglecting an opportunity to speak, no matter how small his audience might be. He addressed himself to all groups: to the great and learned at Paris and elsewhere, as well as to the ignorant and lowly; to those in the religious life and to the laity; to townspeople and to country folk; and to non-Catholics as well as Catholics. St. Francis not only preached frequently, but, according to our standards, he preached long. His reputation was deservedly great and crowds flocked to hear him. The results were likewise great, as is shown by the success of his missionary work in Chablais and by other records of his life. Some of his countless sermons still survive,[1] among them certain shorter ones that became chapters of his treatise

ON THE PREACHER AND PREACHING

On the Love of God.[2] Preaching was indeed one of the means by which the bishop of Geneva attained to sainthood.

Because of his abilities as a speaker and writer, and his great knowledge and his experience with every class of men—all of which he expertly turned to the fulfillment of his duty to spread the gospel—St. Francis de Sales was equipped as few men have been to write on preaching, and has in fact produced the short treatise which is here presented in translation.[3] Its occasion was the departure of a friend, André Frémyot,[4] archbishop of Bourges, to take up residence in his see city. Unable to leave the work of his own diocese and make the long journey to Bourges, St. Francis wrote a letter to the archbishop wishing him well and offering him ideas on this chief duty of a bishop. At the time St. Francis was spending some days in his birthplace, the family chateau at Sales, where, as he remarks in the letter, there were no books to provide him with exact references to the many authors he quotes. It is a long letter, and was written rapidly, and because of such facts the work is all the more spontaneous in expression and all the more noteworthy for the variety and value of its contents. This work is as instructive to us today and as relevant to present-day needs as it was to the man for whom it was first written and to the others who read it more than three hundred and fifty years ago.

André Frémyot was born at Dijon on August 26, 1573, the son of one of the noblest figures of his time, Bénigne Frémyot, Seigneur de Beauregard, father also of Jeanne Françoise Frémyot (1572-1649) who became by marriage the Baroness de Chantal.[5] A holder of high offices in the government at Dijon—he is referred to as President Frémyot because of one of them—M. Frémyot was a firm supporter of Church and throne during the religious wars that ravaged France in the second half of the sixteenth century, and he suffered severely for his loyalty: he had to seek safety in exile, his property was confiscated, and his family was persecuted. When his son André was held hostage by the opposite forces and threatened with death unless the father, then in exile, came over to their side, Bénigne Frémyot gave the great answer: "Il vaut mieux au fils mourir innocent qu' au père vivre perfide." Both father and son became close friends of St. Francis de Sales, and it was in their home in Dijon that St. Francis first met the widowed Mme. de Chantal.

André Frémyot's early education was under the direction of Claude Robert[6] and he later became a student of jurisprudence at the University of Padua, St.

Francis de Sales' *alma mater*, for law. Although thus trained for a legal career, Frémyot was made commendatory abbot of Saint-Etienne de Dijon and later prior of Nantua. He received minor orders and subdiaconate, and while still a subdeacon his name was presented by Cardinal Arnaud d'Ossat[7] to Pope Clement VIII,[8] who preconized him archbishop of Bourges on June 16, 1603. Consecrated in Paris on December 6, 1603, he took possession of his diocese by procurator on December 24, 1603. He did not celebrate his first Mass until Holy Thursday, April 15, 1604, when St. Francis de Sales assisted him at the altar, and it was not until October 24, 1604 that he made his solemn entry into his diocese, or, as St. Francis more realistically puts it, joined his flock.

Archbishop Frémyot was noted for his good works, especially the use of his own means for charitable purposes, and for his patronage of various religious communities. In 1615 he introduced the Capuchins, Augustinians, and Minims into his diocese, in 1617 the Carmelites, and in 1618 the Religious of the Visitation, who had been established in 1610 by his sister and St. Francis de Sales. In addition to certain minor works, he wrote a treatise *De notis ecclesiae*, dedicated to King Henry IV[9] and published in the year of the king's assassination.

Because of political pressure he resigned his see in 1621 and was made abbot of Breteuil, abbot of Ferrières, and later prior of Nogent-le-Rotrou. In 1626 he headed an embassy to Pope Urban VIII, who appointed him commissioner for the process of beatification of the dead bishop of Geneva. He died in Paris on May 13, 1641.

It is easy to picture this young man at the time St. Francis' letter was written to him. Thirty-one years old, the son of a famous father, and heir to wealth and rank, he had been chosen to be bishop of a great French see, although without experience, special training for the priesthood, and perhaps any great inclination to it. The long months between his consecration and first Mass, and the still longer months between appointment and taking up residence in his diocese, are indicative of his state of mind as well as of ecclesiastical procedure in seventeenth-century France. St. Francis must have thought of both the young archbishop's personal needs and those of the faithful at Bourges when he wrote to him about his duty to preach. The letter manifests how ardently St. Francis wanted to help his friend, not only as a preacher, but in other ways as well, and reveals how clearly he saw both Frémyot's limitations and his native talents along with the particular dangers to which he would be exposed.

ON THE PREACHER AND PREACHING

St. Francis' concern for his friend's welfare is further
shown by a letter he sent from Sales to President Frémyot on October 7, 1604.[10] It reads in part:

> M. de Bourges and Mme. de Chantal, your dear
> and worthy children, have undoubtedly been too
> favorable in persuading you to wish me well. From
> the letter you have been pleased to write me I see
> clearly that they have used colors with which my
> poor soul has never been painted. And you, sir, have
> not been less ready or, as I know, less disposed to
> give them ample and generous credence. "Char-
> ity," says the apostle, "believes all things and re-
> joices with the good."[11] In this alone have they
> been unable to go too far in stating, and you, sir,
> in believing, that I have dedicated to them all my
> affections, all of which are thus acquired by you,
> since your children belong to you together with
> whatever they possess.
>
> Permit me, sir, to let my pen run along with my
> thoughts in answering your letter. In very truth,
> I have recognized in M. de Bourges such natural
> goodness of mind and heart that I have allowed
> myself to discuss with him the duties of our com-
> mon vocation with such freedom that, to return to
> myself, I do not know which of us used more sim-
> plicity, he in listening to me or I in speaking to
> him. Sir, friendships founded on Jesus Christ do not
> cease to be reverential for being very simple and in

good faith. We are well cut out to serve one another. Our desires to serve God and his Church—I confess that I have some, and he cannot conceal from me that he is filled with them—have been, I think, sharpened and enlivened by our meeting.

But, sir, you desire that I on my part continue the discussion on this subject by letters. I assure you that even if I wished not to, I could not keep myself from doing this; in fact, I have sent him a letter of four sheets entirely upon this matter.[12] Sir, I take no account of the fact that I am less than he, and that he is more than I am in so many ways. "*Amor aequat amantes.*"[13] I speak sincerely to him, and with all the trust my soul can have in his, which I esteem to be most open, honest, and vigorous in friendship.

If we speak of André Frémyot, aged 31, as a young archbishop, we do not forget that Francis de Sales, his guide, friend, and more than philosopher, was only 37, a priest for but eleven and a bishop for less than two years. Born on August 21, 1567, his birth and rearing were much like those of the archbishop. On both his father's and his mother's side he came from noble stock, and more importantly from a home of firm faith and deep piety. His education was the best that his age could offer, and that is to say much. From private tutors, his teachers at the college of Clermont in Paris and at the university of Padua, and by intense study on his own part, he had acquired the great knowledge and splendid culture that show humanism in its best flowering. For the humanism of St. Francis de Sales is complete: it includes not only the great Greeks and Romans but also the Fathers of the Church, the schoolmen, and the best names of the renaissance and the counter-reformation. To young Francis de Sales belonged all the talents, all the graces of person and manner, all the advantages of wealth and rank, all that nature and society could offer. But above such natural talents and acquisitions, and above the glittering prospects of success and honor in the world, were the truer gifts of grace that he had accepted from God. These latter gifts found their fulfillment when he answered Christ's call to serve him as a priest. Who can think that it was an easy thing to turn his back on the brilliant career that beckoned to him? Who can fail to see that the choice was possible only because of countless hard decisions and heavy sacrifices that he had made in the years before? Soon after his ordination as a priest on December 18, 1593, he began the arduous work of re-evangelizing Chablais, and as part of that task he produced his first writings, the *Controversies* and the *Defense of the Standard of the Holy Cross*.[14] His renown spread to Paris and to Rome as well as to other less famous places. In 1599 Pope Clement VIII named him coadjutor to Claude de Granier, bishop of Geneva, and on December 8, 1602, he was consecrated a bishop and succeeded to the see.

Thus when Francis de Sales wrote his letter of direction and encouragement to his friend, great things had been done but even greater deeds lay ahead. In the eighteen years that were left to him, he produced his two masterpieces, the *Introduction to the Devout Life*[15] and the treatise *On the Love of God*, wrote innumerable letters, preached innumerable sermons, founded with St. Jeanne Françoise Frémyot de Chantal the Religious of the Visitation, carried out diplomatic missions and worked unceasingly for the salvation of souls and to build up his diocese and the Church. Before he died on December 28, 1622, it was clear to those of his time and place that God had put a saint among them, and work on his cause was quickly begun and pushed forward. Thirty-nine years after his death Francis de Sales was declared a *beatus*,[16] and on April 19, 1665 he was canonized by Pope Alexander VII. On July 7, 1877, Pope Pius IX declared him a doctor of the Church.

While the main purpose of the letter is to instruct Archbishop Frémyot on how to preach and to encourage him to fulfill his duty in this regard, it also has sound advice on certain other ideals and duties of the ecclesiastical life. The Aristotelian-scholastic formation of St. Francis' mind is in evidence throughout the treatise. Making effective use of the framework of the four causes,[17] he is able to present in a systematic way the results of his own experience, reading, and reflection upon this burdensome but necessary task. Everything that he says about the material making up a good sermon, the form into which it should be cast, and the final cause of preaching—that its hearers "may have life, and have it more abundantly"[18]—is of value and interest. Having analyzed and commented on preaching according to each of the four causes, St. Francis sums it up in an impressive definition: "To preach is the publication and declaration of God's will, made to men by one lawfully commissioned to that task, to the end of instructing and moving them to serve his divine Majesty in this world so as to be saved in the next."[19]

If a preacher adheres to St. Francis' principles as given in the letter, developed in other writings, and exemplified by his practice, he will turn to Sacred Scripture as the primary and indispensable source of sermon material. St. Paul's injunction, "Preach the word,"[20] tells us what our subjects must be and where to go for what will establish and illustrate them. This scriptural ma-

INTRODUCTION

terial can be interpreted according to the four senses;
namely, the literal, the allegorical, the anagogical, and
the tropological. The lives of the saints are also a great
source of subject matter, because they are simply the
gospel put into practice. Profane history can be used,
but with caution. It is permissible for the preacher to
quote verses from the pagan poets, for St. Paul himself
quotes them, as do the Fathers of the Church. The use
of natural history is both good in itself and authorized
by Scriptural and patristic practice. The writings of
the great theologians, especially St. Thomas Aquinas,
are another mine of sermon material.

Certain things are to be avoided, among them over-
use of allegory, unseemly analogies, and references to
pagan fables. A literary device—or we may more prop-
erly say a literary vice—is pointed out and warned
against; it is the practice of giving elaborate imaginary
descriptions of a Scriptural scene, or worse still of putting fanciful conversations into the mouths of scriptural characters and assigning the speaker's own paltry
ideas to their minds.[21]

St. Francis' views on the proper arrangement of sermon material and how it should be expressed and delivered are of equal worth to those on content. Great
in every way, his high standards as an artist are shown

succinctly but clearly by his insistence that the form into which the preacher casts his matter is of the utmost importance. "Say marvelous things," he points out, "but do not say them well, and they are nothing. Say only a little but say it well, and it is very much." The preacher must be natural, simple, and well prepared, and he must make no pretense to learning that he does not possess; he should be above tricks and affectations in gesture or in speech. He should be sincere and never stoop to flattering those present before him "whether kings, or princes, or popes." He should not preach too long, but for at least half an hour. Above all, everywhere and always he should show his love for those to whom he preaches.

Although the fact is not always observed or sufficiently remarked on, St. Francis de Sales is an immensely learned writer.[22] Because of his thorough education in philosophy, theology, law, and classical literature, and because of native genius, capacity for study, and industry, his knowledge is wide and deep but never obtrusive or used without need. It is after rather than while reading one of his works that we become fully aware of how thoroughly he has documented his teaching and how well he has illustrated it by the works of others. Thus his letter on preaching, written, as he says, with a running pen, out in the country and without use of books, shows itself to be filled with this solid learning. His rule for the preacher holds for himself when he writes on preaching: Sacred Scripture comes first. Twenty-three books—the four gospels, the Acts of the Apostles, eight Pauline epistles, and 1 John in the New Testament, along with nine Old Testament books—are quoted for a total of 65 passages.

Among the Fathers of the Church, Augustine, Ambrose, John Chrysostom, Gregory the Great, and Hilary are cited or referred to, and among medieval thinkers, St. Thomas Aquinas, St. Bernard, St. Antoninus of Florence, and William of Lyons. Later theologians are also recommended, such as Louis of Granada, Stella, Salmeron, Diez, Rossignol, Hylaret, Osorius, and Barradas. A reference to his patron saint is taken from St. Bonaventure's *Life of St. Francis of Assisi*, and the second Franciscan rule is cited. St. Athanasius' account of St. Anthony of Egypt is quoted. St. Charles Borromeo, to whom he had great devotion, is referred to twice. Plutarch's *Lives*, of which he makes frequent use in the treatise *On the Love of God*, are used for reflections on Alexander, Julius Caesar, and Lucretia. Aristotle is quoted and Aratus and Menander are named. The authority of Erasmus is appealed to in the field of teaching and learning, and the *Pontificale Romanum* and the canons of the Council of Trent are cited. All these quotations and references come spontaneously out of the store of knowledge that St. Francis de Sales had built up during his formal studies in Paris and Padua and in even greater measure during the years of incessant reading that followed.

In addition to its mature thought and solid learning, all of which is clearly stated and effectively arranged, the letter has a further quality that leaves its deep impression on us as we read it today. Like whatever St. Francis de Sales put down in writing or put forth in sermons and conferences, it is filled with his love for its reader. We know this from particular statements as well as from the whole spirit and purpose of the letter. "Nothing is impossible to love!" "Heart speaks to heart." "Permit me to write these words of love, because I speak as a Christian." "Consider me as completely your servant as any living man." "To preach well it is sufficient to love well." "Without having a tenth part of your talents, Cardinal Borromeo preached, gave good example, and became a saint." "Never let yourself be carried away by any consideration whatsoever that could stop or hinder you from preaching." "God wills it, and men want it. It is God's glory; it is your salvation." "You can do it, sir, and you must do it." Along with all that St. Francis de Sales tells us in this letter, such words speak today as urgently to Catholic bishops and priests—and by extension to all Catholic teachers—as when they were first addressed to André Frémyot, archbishop of Bourges.

My Lord:

Nothing is impossible to love! I am only a poor, un-couth preacher, but this fact makes me undertake to tell you my ideas on the right way to preach. I do not know if it is your love for me that draws this "water from the rock"[1] or my love for you that causes roses to spring from among thorns. Permit me to write these words of love because I speak as a Christian. Do not find it strange if I offer you both water and roses. Both terms are proper to all Catholic teaching, no matter how badly expressed. I make my start, and ask God to put his helping hand to it.

So as to speak with order, I will discuss preaching in re-lation to its four causes, the efficient, the final, the ma-terial, and the formal;[2] that is, who must preach, the end for which he must preach, what he must preach, and the manner in which he must preach.

I

THE PREACHER[3]

No one should preach except on these three conditions: a good life, good doctrine, and a lawful mission.

I shall say nothing of the preacher's mission or vocation, beyond noting that bishops have not only this mission but likewise its source within their ministry, whereas other preachers have only its rivulets. To preach is their first and their great duty, as is said when they are consecrated.[4] To this effect they receive a special grace at their consecration, and they must render this grace fruitful. In his quality as a bishop St. Paul cries out: "Woe is to me if I do not preach the gospel."[5] The Council of Trent says,[6] "To preach is a bishop's principal duty." Consideration of this fact should encourage us, for in this task God assists us in a special way. It is marvelous what great power a bishop's preaching has in comparison with that of other preachers. Abundant as are the rivulets, men like to drink from the source itself.

With regard to doctrine, it must be sufficient but it is not required that it be extraordinary. St. Francis[7] was not learned; nevertheless he was a great and a good preacher. In our own time the Blessed Cardinal Borromeo[8] possessed only a moderate amount of scientific theology, but still he worked wonders. I know a hundred such examples. A great man of letters—Erasmus,[9] in fact—has said that the best way to acquire knowledge and to become a learned man is to teach. One becomes a preacher by preaching.[10] I wish merely to say this one word: a preacher's knowledge is always sufficient when he has no desire to appear to know more than he actually does. Are we unable to speak well on the mystery of the Trinity? Let us say nothing of it. Are we not sufficiently learned to explain St. John's *"In principio"*?[11] Let us leave it alone. There is no lack of other more useful subjects; there is no question of our doing everything.

With regard to a good life, it is required in the manner that St. Paul states for a bishop, and no more, since there is no need for us to be better in order to be preachers than to be bishops. Hence this requirement has already been established: *"Oportet episcopum esse ir-reprehensibilem,"* says St. Paul.[12]

However, I point out that not only must a bishop and a preacher not be guilty of mortal sin, but also that he must avoid certain venial sins, yes, even certain acts that are in themselves not sinful. St. Bernard, our own doctor, says these words: *"Nugae saecularium sunt blasphemiae clericorum."*[13] A person living in the world can play games, go hunting, and go out at night to pay social visits. There is nothing objectionable in all that, and when done for recreation there is no sin in it. But in a bishop, in a preacher, unless such actions are fenced around by countless circumstances that unhappily are not easy to find, they are scandalous, even very scandalous. People say, "They have their good times. They enjoy themselves to their hearts' content." After that, go out and preach on mortification, and you will be ridiculed. I do not say that one can never take part in any really proper game, once or twice a month by way of recreation, but it should be done with great circumspection.

Hunting is absolutely forbidden.[14] I say the same thing as to needless spending on banquets, clothing, and books.[15] Among people living in the world such things are superfluous expenditures, but among bishops they

25

are grave sins. St. Bernard instructs us when he says:[16] *"Clamant pauperes post nos: 'Nostrum est quod expenditis, nobis crudeliter eripitur quidquid inaniter expenditur.'"* How can we reprimand the extravagant ways of the world if we make a show of our own?

St. Paul says,[17] *"Oportet episcopum esse hospitalem."* Hospitality does not consist in putting on banquets but in gladly receiving people at such a table as a bishop ought to maintain and the Council of Trent regulates:[18] *"Oportet mensam episcoporum esse frugalem."* I except certain occasions that prudence and charity can easily recognize.

Furthermore, we must never preach without having celebrated Mass or wishing to celebrate it. According to St. Chrysostom,[19] it is beyond belief how demons dread the mouth that has received Holy Communion, and it is true. I think that we can say with St. Paul,[20] *"An experimentum quaeritis ejus qui loquitur in me Christus?"* One has much greater assurance, fervor, and light. *"Quamdiu sum in mundo, lux sum mundi,"* says the Savior.[21] It is certain that since our Lord is really within us, he gives us brightness, for he is the light.[22] Also, after the disciples at Emmaus had communicated, "their eyes were opened."[23] At the very least, we must go to confession, in keeping with what God tells us, as reported by David,[24] "*Peccatori autem dixit Deus: Quare tu enarras justitias meas et assumis testamentum meum per ostium?*" And St. Paul says:[25] "*Castigo corpus meum et in servitutem redigo, ne cum aliis praedicaverim ipse reprobus efficiar.*" But this is more than enough on this point.

II

LIGHT AND WARMTH

THE END is the master cause among all things.[1] It is the end that moves the agent to act, for every agent acts both for an end[2] and according to an end. It is the end that determines the extent of both matter and form: according to our design to build a large house or a small one we prepare materials for it and provide for its construction.

What then is the end of the preacher in the act of preaching? His end and intention must be to do what our Lord came into this world to do. Here is what he himself says[3] in this regard: "*Ego veni ut vitam habeant, et abundantius habeant.*" Therefore, the preacher's end is that sinners dead in iniquity may live to justice, and that just men, who possess spiritual life, "may have it more abundantly" and become more and more perfect,

31

and also, as was said to Jeremias,[4] *"ut evellas et destruas"* vices and sins, *"et aedificas et plantes"* virtues and perfections. Hence when the preacher is in the pulpit, he must say in his heart, *"Ego veni ut isti vitam habeant, et abundantius habeant."*[5]

To achieve this purpose and plan, the preacher must do two things, namely, instruct and move. He must teach about virtues and vices: about virtues, so as to make men love, desire, and practise them; about vices so as to make them detest, struggle against, and fly from them. To sum it all up, the preacher must bring light to the intellect and warmth to the will.[6] For this reason God sent down on the apostles on Pentecost day—this was the day of their episcopal consecration, for they had already been ordained priests on the day of the Last Supper[7]—"tongues of fire,"[8] so that they would know that a bishop's tongue must enlighten his hearers' intellects and warm their wills.[9]

I know that many writers say that, thirdly, the preacher must give delight. For myself, I make a distinction and say that there is a delight that follows upon learning and the movement of the will. What soul is so unfeeling that it does not take very great pleasure from learning the path to heaven in so good and holy a way, and does not feel the greatest consolation in love of

LIGHT AND WARMTH

God? Such delight must be brought about; however, it is not distinct from teaching and moving but dependent on them. There is another kind of delight which does not depend on teaching and moving but produces its effect apart from teaching and moving and very often prevents them. This is a sort of tickling of ears, which derives from a certain secular, worldly, and profane elegance and from various affectations and arrangements of ideas, words, and phrases. In brief, it depends wholly on artifice. With regard to such pleasure, I strongly and firmly deny that a preacher should even think of it. It must be left to orators out in the world and to tricksters and flatterers who may amuse themselves with it. They do not preach "Jesus Christ crucified";[10] they preach themselves. "*Non sectamur lenocinia rhetorum, sed veritates piscatorum.*"[11]

St. Paul detests hearers who are "*prurientes auribus*,"[12] and as a consequence he detests preachers who desire to please them. Such desire is a form of pedantry. I would not like people to say at the end of a sermon: "What a great orator he is!" "What a wonderful memory he has!" "How learned he is!" "How well he speaks!" I would rather have them say: "How beautiful is repentance!" "How necessary it is!" "How good you are, O my God, how just!" and similar things. Or

33

ON THE PREACHER AND PREACHING

I would prefer that a hearer whose heart has been touched would testify to the preacher's power solely by his amendment of life. *"Ut vitam habeant, et abundantius habeant!"*[13]

III
THE WORD OF GOD

Sᴛ. Pᴀᴜʟ says to Timothy in one sentence: *"Praedica verbum."*[1] We must preach the word of God. *"Praedicate evangelium,"* says the Master.[2] St. Francis explains this when he commands his friars to preach on virtues and vices and on hell and paradise.[3] There is sufficient matter in Sacred Scripture for all of that; nothing further is needed.

Is there no need then to make use of Christian doctors and the writings of the saints? It is indeed necessary to do so. What else is the doctrine of the Fathers of the Church except the gospel explained and Holy Scripture expounded? In other words, the difference between Sacred Scripture and the teaching of the Fathers is like that between a whole almond and an almond cracked open so that the nut can be eaten by anyone, or like that between a whole loaf of bread and a loaf broken into pieces and distributed. On the contrary, therefore, it is necessary to make use of such works, for they have been instruments by which God has communicated to us the true meaning of his word.

Can we make use of the lives of the saints? Why, good heavens, is there anything as useful, anything as good as they are? Moreover, what else is the life of a saint except the gospel put into practice? There is no more difference between the written gospel and the lives of the saints than between music set down in notes and music that is sung.

What about events in profane history? They are good but we must use them as we do mushrooms, that is, in very small amounts and only to sharpen the appetite, and even so they must be well prepared. As St. Jerome says,[4] we must do to them what the Israelites did to the captive women whom they wished to marry. It is necessary to pare down their nails and cut off their hair;[5] that is, to bring them completely into the service of the gospel and true Christian virtue. We must remove whatever is blameworthy in such pagan and profane deeds and separate *"pretiosum a vili,"* as Holy Writ says.[6] In considering Caesar's great character his ambition must be singled out and remarked on; in Alexander's, his vanity, arrogance, and pride; in Lucretia's chastity, her death in despair.[7]

What about the fables told by the poets? From them, choose nothing whatsoever, unless it is very brief and very relevant, and given such a setting as a counterbalance that everyone will see that we have no wish to profess such things. All this should be done as briefly as possible. Verses taken from the poets are useful. At times older writers, devout as they were, quoted them, even as late as St. Bernard, but where he learned them I do not know.[8] St. Paul was the first to cite Aratus[9] and Menander.[10] But with regard to fables, I have never met them in any sermon by the Fathers, except a single reference to Ulysses and the sirens made by St. Ambrose in one of his sermons.[11] This is why I say, use either nothing whatsoever or practically nothing. It is not fitting to place the idol of Dagon in the Ark of the Covenant.[12]

What about natural history?[13] This is excellent, for the world, made by God's word, manifests every part of that word. All its parts sing the praises of its maker. It is a book containing God's word, but in a language that not every man understands.[14] Those who understand it by way of meditation exert great efforts to make use of it, as did St. Anthony,[15] who had no other library.

ON THE PREACHER AND PREACHING

St. Paul says,[16] "*Invisibilia Dei per ea quae facta sunt intellecta conspiciuntur*," and David states,[17] "*Caeli enarrant gloriam Dei.*" This book is good for similitudes, for comparisons "*a minori ad majus*,"[18] and for thousands of other things. The ancient Fathers are filled with them, and in a thousand passages Holy Scripture says: "*Vade ad formicam*;"[19] "*Sicut gallina congregat pullos suos*;"[20] "*Quemadmodum desiderat cervus*;"[21] "*Quasi struthio in deserto*;"[22] "*Videte lilia agri*;"[23] and a hundred thousand similar things.

Above all the preacher must be on guard against relating false miracles, foolish stories, such as certain visions drawn from certain low grade authors, and indecent things that can render our ministry deserving of scorn and criticism.[24]

The foregoing is what in my opinion relates to the matter in general; it remains to speak in detail about the various parts of a sermon.

The first part of such matter is made up of scriptural passages, which truly hold first place and constitute the foundation of the structure. In the last analysis we preach the word, and our doctrine rests on authority.[25] "*Ipse dixit*.[26] *Haec dicit Dominus*,"[27] the prophets say. Our Lord himself states,[28] "*Doctrina mea non est mea, sed ejus qui misit me.*" But as far as possible the passages must be interpreted very naturally and clearly. Now, we can make good use of Scripture by explaining such passages in one of the four ways that the ancients have indicated:

> *Littera facta docet; quid credas, allegoria;*
> *Quid speres, anagoge; quid agas, tropologia.*[29]

This couplet does not have too much in the way of good quantity, but it has some rhyme and still more reason.

THE LITERAL OR HISTORICAL SENSE

As to the literal sense, preaching must be based on the commentaries of the doctors; this is all that can be said about it. However, it is up to the preacher to evaluate it and to weigh the words, their propriety, and their emphasis. For example, yesterday in this village[30] I explained the commandment: *"Diliges Dominum Deum tuum ex toto corde, ex tota anima, ex tota mente."*[31] With our own St. Bernard[32] I thought that *"ex toto corde"* means courageously, valiantly, and fervently, since courage pertains to the heart. *"Ex tota anima"* means with affection, because the soul, in that it is the soul, is the source of passions and affections. "*Ex tota mente*" means spiritually and prudently, because "*mens*" is spirit and the superior part of the soul, and to it belong discretion and judgment to have zeal "*secundum scientiam et discretionem*."[33] Thus the word "*diligere*" must be considered since it comes from "*eligo*"[34] and naturally represents the literal sense, viz., that our heart, our soul, and our spirit should choose and prefer God above all things. This is that true appreciative love of which theologians interpret these words.

When there is a difference of opinion among the Fathers we should refrain from bringing forward opinions that must be refuted, since no one mounts the pulpit to dispute against the Catholic Fathers and doctors. There is no need to reveal the weakness of our teachers[35] and what slips they make as men, "*ut sciant gentes quoniam homines sunt*."[36] However, we can rightly set forth various interpretations, praising and evaluating all of them one after the other, as I did during the past Lent with the six opinions and interpretations of the Fathers of these words: "*Dicite quia servi inutiles sumus*,"[37] and with these other words, "*Non est meum dare vobis*."[38] If you recall, I drew certain very good conclusions from each of them, but I think I passed over that of St. Hilary. Or if I did not, I was wrong and should have done so, because it is not a probable interpretation.[39]

THE ALLEGORICAL SENSE

With regard to the allegorical sense, the preacher must observe four or five points. The first is to take an allegorical sense that is not too far-fetched, as do those who make allegories of everything. It must be taken in a natural manner, in harmony with the literal meaning, as St. Paul does[40] when he allegorically takes Esau and Jacob for the Jewish people and the Gentiles,[41] and Sion or Jerusalem for the Church.[42]

Secondly, where it is not really apparent that one thing is the figure of the other, we must not treat such things as if one were a figure of the other, but simply by way of comparison. For example, many allegorically interpret the juniper tree under which Elias slept in his distress[43] as a figure of the Cross. Personally, I prefer to put it thus: just as Elias slept under the juniper tree, so ought we to take repose under our Lord's Cross in the sleep of holy meditation, and not in this fashion:

just as Elias signifies the Christian, so the juniper signifies the Cross. I would not like to assert that one signifies the other, but would prefer to compare the one to the other. In this way the discourse is more solid and less subject to criticism.

Thirdly, it is necessary that the allegory be becoming. In this regard many men are blameworthy when they allegorize the command in Deuteronomy, chapter 25,[44] that a woman must not seize a man by the private parts: "*Si habuerunt inter se jurgium viri duo, et unus contra alterum rixari coeperit, volensque uxor alterius eruere et apprehenderit verenda ejus, abscides manum illius, nec flecteris super eam ulla misericordia.*" They say that she represents the evil that makes the Synagogue reproach the Gentiles for their origin and for the fact that they were not children of Abraham. This may have some apparent truth, but it is unbecoming because the command given arouses dangerous images in the hearer's mind.

Fourthly, we must not make over-elaborate allegories, as they lose their persuasive power by their length and seem affected.

Fifthly, the application must be made clearly and with good judgment so as to relate skillfully the various parts to one another.

THE WORD OF GOD

We must observe the same rules with regard to the anagogical and tropological senses. Of these two, the anagogical sense relates scriptural stories to what will take place in the next life, while the tropological sense relates them to what obtains in the soul and conscience. I will give an example that will serve for all four senses.

"Duae gentes sunt in utero tuo, et duo populi ex utero tuo dividentur, populusque populum superabit, et majori serviet minori."[45]

These words of God, who is speaking of Esau and Jacob in Genesis 25, literally mean that two nations issue according to the flesh, that of Esau and that of Jacob, namely, the Idumeans and the Israelites, and that the lesser of the two, which was the nation of the Israelites, would surpass the greater and elder, which was the people of Idumea, in the time of David.

Allegorically, Esau represents the Jewish people, which was the elder in knowledge of salvation, for the Jews were preached to first. Jacob represents the Gentiles, who were younger; nevertheless the Gentiles in the end surpassed the Jews.

Anagogically, Esau represents the body, which is

the elder, for before the soul was created, the body was made both in Adam and in us.[46] Jacob signifies spirit, which is younger. In the other life the spirit will surpass and dominate the body, which will completely serve the soul without any contradiction.

Tropologically, Esau is self-love, while Jacob is love of God in our soul. Self-love is the elder, for it is born with us; love of God is the younger, because it is acquired by the sacraments and repentance. Still it is of necessity that love of God is the master, and when it is in the soul, self-love serves it and is its inferior.

These four senses provide great, good, and elevated material for our preaching, and marvelously add to understanding the doctrine taught. For this reason it is necessary to make use of them, but under the same conditions that I have said are requisite for using the allegorical sense.

After scriptural pronouncements those taken from the Fathers and the councils hold second rank. With regard to them, I say merely that except on very rare occasions we must choose brief, pointed, powerful passages. Preachers who make long citations detract both from their own fervor and from the attention of most of their hearers. They also expose themselves to the danger of loss of memory. Short, strong sentences are those like this one from St. Augustine, *"Qui fecit te sine te, non salvabit te sin te"*;[47] and another, *"Qui poenitentibus veniam promisit, tempus poenitendi non promisit,"*[48] and the like. In our own St. Bernard there is an unlimited number of such passages. But if they have been quoted in Latin, it is necessary for good effect to say them in French and to give them full value by restating them and clearly drawing out their consequences.

THE APPEAL TO REASON

Next come the rational arguments that a noble nature and good mind can very effectively employ. With regard to such arguments, they are more easily found among the doctors, and especially St. Thomas, than anywhere else. Since they are well worked out, they provide extremely good material. If you wish to speak on one of the virtues, turn to the index to St. Thomas,[49] see where he speaks of it, and consider what he has to say. You will find many arguments that will serve you for material. Finally, one must not employ such material unless it can be made very clearly understood, at least by ordinary hearers.

ON THE PREACHER AND PREACHING

The Use of Illustration

Illustrations have wonderful power and add great savor to a sermon. It is only necessary that they be proper, well expressed, and better applied. It is necessary to choose suitable, outstanding episodes, to narrate them clearly and distinctly, and to apply them in a striking way, as the Fathers do when they set forth the example of Abraham about to sacrifice his own son,[50] so as to show that we should shirk nothing to fulfill God's will. They point out everything that can exalt Abraham's obedience. Abraham, they say, was old, Abraham who had but this one son, so handsome, so wise and virtuous, and so worthy of love. Nevertheless, without making any answer, without any murmur or hesitation, he led his son up the mountain and was ready to sacrifice him with his own hands. In fact, they make this application in a still more vivid way. And thou, O Christian, thou art so hard, so cold, so hesitant to make any sacrifice, I do not say of thy son or daughter, or of thy goods or of some great project, but of a single dollar to relieve the poor for love of God, of a single hour from your leisure in order to serve God, of a single affection, and the like.

But it is necessary to be on guard against making worthless, flabby descriptions, as do many scholars who, in place of proposing a story naturally and for its moral, set out to describe Isaac's beauty, Abraham's sharp sword, the surroundings of the sacrificial place, and similar irrelevant details. One must be neither so brief that the example makes no impression nor so long that it grows tiresome.

We must be on guard against introducing conversations between characters in the episodes unless they are in words taken from Scripture or very probable.[51] For instance, in this story if someone introduces Isaac lamenting over the altar, and imploring his father's mercy so as to escape death, or even Abraham groaning and arguing with himself, he injures and detracts from the strength and resolution of both the one and the other. Thus those who have found such conversations while at meditation should observe two rules in their preaching: one is to see if they rest on a solid foundation of manifest probability; the other is not to set them out at too great length, as that causes coldness in both preacher and hearer.

The examples of the saints are admirable, especially those belonging to the province where one is preaching, as with St. Bernard at Dijon.

Comparisons

It remains to say a few words on comparisons. They have an inestimable efficacy to enlighten the understanding and move the will. We take them from human actions, passing from one act to another, as, for instance, from what shepherds do to what bishops and pastors ought to do, as does our Lord in the parable of the lost sheep.[52] Or we take them from the natural history of herbs, plants, and animals, from philosophy, and in fine from everything. Comparisons based on ordinary things are excellent if they are carefully applied, as our Lord does in the parable of the seed.[53] In those taken from natural history there is a twofold luster if both the history and the application are good, like the scriptural comparison of the renewal or rejuvenation of the eagle[54] with our repentance.

There is a secret in doing this that is extremely helpful to the preacher. This is to take our scriptural comparisons from certain places where few people know how to recognize them. This is done by meditation on the words.

For example, when David speaks of the worldly man, he says, "*Periit memoria eorum cum sonitu.*"[55] I have

THE WORD OF GOD

taken two comparisons from two things that perish together with their sound. When we break a piece of
glass, even as it is broken it perishes while making a
sound. So also the wicked perish with a little noise: men
speak of them at their death. But just as the broken glass
remains altogether useless, so also these unfortunate men
without hope of salvation remain lost forever. The other
comparison is this: when a very rich man dies, they ring
all the bells and great funeral ceremonies are held over
him. But with the passing sound of the bells, who gives
him a blessing? Who refers to him? No one. Speaking
of a man who had no charity but performed certain
deeds, St. Paul says that he became like "sounding brass
or a tinkling cymbal."[56] We can make a comparison
from the bell that calls others to church but does not
enter there itself. So also the man who does certain
deeds without charity edifies others and urges them on
to paradise but he himself does not enter into it.

To find such comparisons, it is necessary to consider
whether the words are metaphorical, for when they are
such, there is a comparison right away for anyone who
knows how to recognize it. For example, "*Viam man-
datorum tuorum cucurri cum dilatasti cor meum.*"[57]
Here we must reflect on the words "*dilatasti*" and
"*cucurri,*" for each of them is used metaphorically.

Next it is necessary to look at things that move more quickly because of dilatation, and you will find some of them, such as ships when the wind fills out their sails. As soon as a propitious wind seizes the sails of ships lying in port, fills them, and makes them swell, they set out. So also with men. When the favorable wind of the Holy Spirit enters into our heart, our soul moves and sails over the sea of the commandments. In fact, whoever observes this rule will profitably fashion many fine comparisons. In such comparisons we must observe the proprieties and never say anything vile, base, or coarse.

After all this I advise you that we can use such scriptural applications to great advantage, even though often what we draw from Scripture may not be the true meaning. Thus St. Francis says[58] that alms are *"panis angelorum"*[59] because the angels procure them by their inspirations, and he applies this passage: *"Panem angelorum manducavit homo."*[60] In this we must be careful and restrained.

The Homiletic Method

We must adhere to method in all things; there is nothing that is more helpful to a preacher, makes his preaching more profitable, and is so pleasing to his hearers. I hold that his method should be clear and evident, and in no wise hidden, as it is with many preachers who think that it is a mighty master stroke to make sure that no one will recognize their method. I ask you, what good is a method if no one sees it and the hearer does not recognize it?

To help you in this regard, I will discuss it with you, whether you wish to preach on some story, such as the Nativity, Resurrection, or Assumption, some scriptural text, such as *"Omnis qui se exaltat humiliabitur,"*[61] an entire gospel,[62] or various texts, or the life of a saint together with a text.

When we preach on an historical event, we can use one of these methods: (1) Consider how many persons there are in the story you wish to preach on, and then draw some reflection from each of them. For example, in the Resurrection I see the women named Mary, the angels, the guards at the sepulcher, and our dear Savior. In the Marys I see fervor and care; in the angels, joy and jubilation in their white garments and brightness; in the guards I see the weakness of men who act against God; in Jesus I see glory, triumph over death, and hope of our own resurrection.

(2) One can take up the principal point in a mystery,

such as the Resurrection in our preceding example, and then consider what precedes and follows this point. The Resurrection was preceded by death and descent into hell, the deliverance of the Fathers who were in Abraham's bosom, and the Jews' fear that some one would steal the body. The Resurrection itself is in a blessed and glorious body. What follows is the earthquake, the coming and appearance of the angels, the search by the women, and the angels' response. In all these parts there are marvels to relate and in good order.

(3) In all mysteries we can consider the following points: who? why? and how? Who arises? Our Lord. Why? For his glory and our good. How? Glorious, immortal, and so on. Who is born? the Savior. Why? To save us. How? Poor, naked, cold, in a stable, as a little child.

(4) After setting forth the story in brief paraphrase, we can sometimes draw from it two or three considerations. The first is what we must learn in order to build up our faith; the second, to increase our hope; the third, to enflame our charity; the fourth, for imitation and practice.[63] In the example of the Resurrection, for faith, we see God's omnipotence: a body passes through stone and becomes immortal, impassible, and completely spiritualized. We see how it is that we must firmly be-

lieve that in the Blessed Sacrament this same body does not occupy a place, cannot be injured by the breaking of the species, and is there in a spiritual and yet real way. For hope, if Jesus Christ is risen we will arise, says St. Paul.[64] He has opened the path for us. For charity, completely risen as he is, he still remains on earth to instruct the Church, and for our welfare he delays taking possession of heaven, the true place of risen bodies.[65] Ah, what love! For our imitation: he arose on the third day. O God, shall not we arise by contrition, satisfaction, and confession? He shatters the stone; let us vanquish all difficulties.

OTHER METHODS

When you wish to preach on a text, you must reflect on what virtue it refers to, as for example, *"Qui se humiliat exaltabitur."*[66] Here it is very evident that the subject is humility. However, there are other texts where the subject is not so obvious, as *"Quomodo huc intrasti non habens vestem nuptialem?"*[67] Here the virtue is charity, but you see it covered over by a garment, for charity is the nuptial garment. Hence when you have discovered in the text you wish to discuss the virtue it indicates, you can reduce your sermon to method, considering in what the virtue consists, its true marks, its effects, and the means of acquiring or practising it. This has always been my own method, and I have been consoled at finding that the book by Father Rossignol, S.J., adheres to the same method. His book is entitled *De actionibus virtutum*, and is printed at Venice.[68] It will be very useful to you.

There is another method, showing how the virtue treated is worthy of honor, useful, and delightful or pleasing, which are the three goods that can be desired. One can treat it in still another way; namely, to point out the goods that the virtue gives and the evils that the contrary vice brings on us. However, the first method is the most useful.

When we discuss a gospel containing many statements, it is necessary to consider those on which we wish to dwell, see what virtues they treat, speak briefly about them in the way I have stated for a single text, and run through and paraphrase the others. However, this method of covering an entire gospel containing various statements is less fruitful. The preacher can dwell for only a little while on each one, he cannot separate them effectively, nor can he instruct his hearers as he would like.

When one discusses the life of a saint the method is different. That which I employed in my funeral oration over M. de Mercoeur[69] is good because it is St. Paul's. *"Ut 'pie' erga Deum, 'sobrie' erga seipsum, 'juste' erga proximum vixerit."*[70] It reports the parts of the saint's life each in its own place. Or it is well to consider what the saint accomplished *"agendo,"*[71] namely, his virtues; *"patiendo,"*[72] namely, his sufferings, whether by martyrdom or by mortification; *"orando,"*[73] namely, his miracles. Or it is helpful to consider how he fought against the devil, the world, and the flesh; that is, against pride, avarice, and concupiscence. This is the division made by St. John, who says:[74] *"Omne quod est in mundo est concupiscentia carnis, etc.,"* Again, we can consider, as I did at Fontaines[75] on St. Bernard, how we must honor God in his saint and the saint in God, how we must serve God in imitation of his saint, how we must pray to God through his saint's intercession. To do this is to survey the life of the saint we speak of, and to put everything in its proper place.

There are plenty of ways to begin, and after a little practice you will find others which will be suitable and better for yourself. With regard to method it remains for us to say that I readily place scriptural passages in the first place, proofs in the second, similitudes in the third, and in the fourth examples, provided they are sacred, for if profane they are not suitable for closing a discourse. A sacred discourse must be brought to an end with what is sacred. *Item*, method means that from its beginning to the middle a sermon teaches the hearer, and from the middle to the end it moves him. For this reason the affective passages must be placed at the end.

CONTENT PREPARATION

But after all this, I still must tell you how necessary it is to fill out the points of your sermon, and to see how to do so. For example, you are discussing the virtue of humility, and have arranged your points in this way: (1) in what this virtue consists; (2) its marks; (3) its effects; (4) the way to acquire it. This is your arrangement. To acquire ideas you will look up in the authors' indexes the words "*humilitas*," "*humilis*," "*superbia*," and "*superbus*,"[76] and see what the authors say about them. When you have found their descriptions or definitions, you will put them under the heading "In what this virtue consists," and you will endeavor to clarify this point by showing in what the opposite vice consists.

To fill out the second point, you will note in the index

"*humilitas ficta*," "*humilitas indiscreta*,"[77] and the like, by them you will show the difference between true and false humility. If there are examples of one or the other, you will employ them. So also for the other two points. "*Intelligenti pauca.*"[78]

Authors in whom such material is found are St. Thomas,[79] St. Antoninus,[80] Bishop William of Lyons[81] in his *Summa de virtutibus et vitiis*, the *Summa praedicantium* by Philip Diez,[82] and also all his sermons, Osorius,[83] Granada's[84] spiritual works, Hylaret's[85] sermons, Stella's[86] commentary on Luke, and the Jesuits Salmeron[87] and Barradas[88] on the Gospels. St. Gregory[89] excels among the ancients, and there are St. Chrysostom[90] and St. Bernard.[91]

It is necessary for me to give my own opinion. Among all those who have written sermons, Diez pleases me in the highest degree. He acts in good faith, has the spirit of preaching, teaches effectively, explains passages well, offers fine allegories and similitudes and vivid descriptions, takes opportunity to speak admirably, and is very devout and clear. He lacks what is found in Osorius; namely, order and method, for he does not keep to them. But I think it necessary to familiarize yourself with him at the beginning. I say this not because I have made much use of his work, as I have not seen it for a long time, but because I believe it to be such, and I think that I am not mistaken. There is a Spaniard who has written a large book called *Sylva allegoriarum*,[92] which is very useful to anyone who knows how to use it, as are also Benedicti's *Concordances*.[93] This, I think, is the chief part of what I now recall with regard to matter.

IV

HOW WE MUST PREACH

S<small>IR</small>, at this point I desire fuller trust than elsewhere, because I do not hold the common opinion, but still what I say is the very truth.

Form, the philosopher says,[1] gives being and soul to a thing. Say marvelous things, but do not say them well, and they are nothing. Say only a little but say it well, and it is very much. How then must we speak when we preach?[2] We must be on guard against the *"quam-quams"* and the long periodic sentences of the pedants, against their gestures, their airs, and their movements. All such things are the plague of preaching. Preaching must be spontaneous, dignified, courageous, natural, sturdy, devout, serious, and a little slow. But to make it such what must be done? In a word, it means to speak with affection and devotion, with simplicity and candor, and with confidence, and to be convinced of the doctrine we teach and of what we persuade. The supreme art is to have no art. Our words must be set aflame, not by shouts and unrestrained gestures, but by inward affection. They must issue from our heart rather than from our mouth. We must speak well, but heart speaks to heart, and the tongue speaks only to men's ears.

I said that our preaching must be a spontaneous action, in contrast to the constrained and studied action of the pedants. I said dignified, in contrast to the rustic ways of some preachers who make a show of striking their fists, feet, and stomach against the pulpit, shout and utter howls that are strange and often improper. I said courageous in contrast to those who have a certain fearful way of acting as if they were speaking to their fathers and not to their pupils and children. I said natural, in contrast to all artificiality and affectation. I said sturdy, in contrast to a kind of dead, soft, ineffectual action. I said devout, to avoid obsequious and worldly acts of flattery. I said serious, in contrast to those who doff their caps so many times to the audience, make so many signs of respect, and perform so many little tricks by showing their hands or surplices, and making other such indecorous movements. I said a little slow, to avoid a kind of curt and brusque way that diverts the eyes rather than pierces the heart.

I say the same thing about language. It must be clear, simple, and natural, without display of Greek, Hebrew, novel, or fancy words. The structure must be natural, and without prefatory and ornamental phrases. I approve of saying "firstly," "on the first point," and "secondly," "on the second point," so that the people may see the order followed.

I think that no one, and especially no bishop, should resort to flattery of those present, whether they are kings, princes, or popes. There are certain proper ways of gaining good will that the preacher can sometimes use when he speaks to his own people. I am convinced that we make plain our desire for the people's good when we commence with salutations and blessings, and by our wish to be able to help them to salvation. So also as to our country. This must be done briefly, sincerely, and without ornate phrases. The early Fathers, and all those who have been fruitful, abstained from all affectation and worldly ornament. They speak heart to heart, soul to soul, like good fathers speaking to their children. Our usual appellations should be "my brethren," "my people" (if they are yours), "my dear people" or "Christian hearers."

ON THE PREACHER AND PREACHING

The bishop should give the blessing at the end, wearing his mitre, and when this is done he should greet the people. One should finish with some brief but more animated and vigorous words. I approve that on most occasions repetition or recapitulation be given, after which one says four or five fervent words, either in the form of prayer or exhortation. It is well to have certain familiar exclamations ready to be pronounced and employed judiciously: "O God," "the goodness of God," "O good God," "Lord God," "True God," "Eh," "Alas," "Ah," and "my God."

As to preparation, I am in favor of making it in the evening, and in the morning of meditating within oneself on what one wishes to say to others. Preparation made before the Blessed Sacrament has great efficacy according to Granada,[3] and I believe him.

I like preaching that issues from love of neighbor rather than from indignation at them, even in the case of the Huguenots, whom we must treat with great compassion, not flattering them but lamenting over them.

It is always best that our preaching be short rather than long. In this matter I have been at fault up to the present time; I pray that I may correct this. Provided that the sermon lasts a half hour, it cannot be too short.

HOW WE MUST PREACH

If possible, there is no need to give evidence of dis-satisfaction, at least not of anger, as I did on the feast of our Lady, when they rang the bell before I had finished.[4] This was a fault, without doubt along with many others. I do not like jokes and familiarities; they are out of place.

I end by saying that to preach is the publication and declaration of God's will, made to men by one lawfully commissioned to that task, to the end of instructing and moving them to serve his divine Majesty in this world so as to be saved in the next.[5]

V

A PERSONAL APPEAL

Sɪʀ, what will you say to this? Forgive me, I beg of you. I have written with a running pen, without care as to words or art, carried along by my sole desire to testify how obedient I am to you. I have not cited the authors whom I have quoted in certain passages, because I am out in the country where I do not have them at hand. I have also quoted myself, because you want my opinion and not that of others. Since I follow it, why should I not express it?

Before I close this letter I must beseech you, sir, not to let it be seen by anyone whose eyes are less favorable to me than your own. I add my most humble supplication that you never let yourself be carried away by any consideration whatsoever that could stop or hinder you from preaching. The sooner you begin, the sooner you will succeed. Preach often; there is need only for this to become a master. You can do it, sir, and you must do it. You have a good voice; you have sufficient learning; your bearing is correct; your rank in the Church illustrious. God wills it, and men want it. It is God's glory; it is your salvation. Act boldly, sir, and take courage out of love for God.

Without having a tenth part of your talents, Cardinal Borromeo[1] preached, gave good example, and became a saint. We must not seek our own honor, but that of God. Let it be, and God will seek for ours. Start out, sir, at one time when Holy Orders are conferred, at another when Holy Communion is administered. Say four words, then eight, and then a dozen, until you speak for half an hour, and then mount the pulpit. Nothing is impossible to love. Our Lord did not ask St. Peter, "Are you learned or eloquent?" in order to tell him, "*Pasce oves meas*," but "*Amas me?*"[2] To love well is sufficient for speaking well. When St. John was dying he could only repeat a hundred times within a quarter of an hour, "My children, love one another."[3] Provided thus, he went up into the pulpit. But we are scrupulous at mounting there if we do not have marvelous eloquence! Let them talk who cite the great abilities of

your predecessor.[4] He once started out just like yourself.

But, sir, what will you say about me who write to
you in this simple fashion? Love cannot keep silent
where the interests of one we love are involved. Sir, I
have sworn fidelity to you, and one puts up with much
from a faithful and devoted servant. You go, sir, to join
your flock, and I wish it were possible for me to hasten
to assist you there, as I had the honor of doing at your
first Mass.[5] I will accompany you by my prayers and
desires. Your people are waiting to see you, and to be
seen again and again by you. By the beginning they will
pass judgment on the rest. Begin at an early hour to do
what you must always do. Ah, how edified they will
be when they see you often at the altar offering sacrifice for their salvation, and together with your clergy
working for their betterment, speaking from the pulpit
on "the word of reconciliation,"[6] and preaching to
them!

Sir, I am never at the altar without remembering you
to our Lord, and I will be more than happy if I am
worthy of sometimes being kept in your memory. I am,
and throughout my life I shall be, in heart, soul, and
spirit,

ON THE PREACHER AND PREACHING

Sir,

Your most humble servant, and your least and most obedient brother,

Francis, Bishop of Geneva

October 5, 1604

I felt ashamed as I reread this letter, and if it were shorter I would do it over again. However, I have so much confidence in your solid good will that here it is, sir, such as it is. Out of love for God, keep me always in your love, and consider me as completely your servant as any living man, for such I am.

Notes

DEDICATION

The words *"summo ingenio scientia copia"* and *"flumen orationis aureum fundens"* are from Cicero, the first from *Tusculan Disputations*, I, iv, and the second from *Academica*, II, 38. Cicero writes both phrases in praise of Aristotle.

INTRODUCTION

1. Cf. *Oeuvres*, Vols. VII-X.
2. St. Francis de Sales, *On the Love of God*. Translated with an introduction and notes by John K. Ryan. 2 vols. (Garden City, N. Y.: Image Books, 1963). Cf. St. Francis' introduction, I, 46, 47, and the translator's introduction, I, 23. The reader of *On the Love of God* will recognize the homiletic origin of certain chapters.
3. Cf. Letter CCXXIX, "A Monseigneur André Frémyot, Archevêque de Bourges," *Oeuvres*, XII, 299-325.
4. The following biographical material on Archbishop Frémyot and his father, President Bénigne Frémyot, is largely based on the notes in the Annecy edition.

5. At her husband's death in a hunting accident in 1600, Mme. de Chantal was left with four children, a son and three daughters, one of whom married Bernard de Sales, younger brother of St. Francis. The son, Baron Celse-Bénigne de Rabutin Chantal (1595-1627), became one of the most daring soldiers of his time; he was fatally wounded fighting against the English during their attack on the island of Ré. He was married to Marie de Coulanges; their only child lived to become Mme. de Sévigné (1626-1696), great among the names of seventeenth-century French letters and a continuer of the devotion of her grandmother.

When fifteen-year old Celse-Bénigne was about to set out for court, St. Francis wrote to him one of his most interesting letters of spiritual advice. Cf. *Oeuvres*, XIV, 376-81, and Elizabeth Stopp, translator and editor, *St. Francis de Sales, Selected Letters* (London: Faber and Faber, 1960), pp. 186-90. Cf. also Herold J. Heagney, *Madame de Chantal* (New York: P. J. Kenedy and Sons, 1950).

6. Claude Robert (1564-1636) vicar general and archdeacon of Langres, and later author of *Gallia christiana*. Cf. *Catholic Encyclopedia* article *Gallia christiana* and H. Hurter, *Nomenclator litterarius*, 4 vols. (Innsbruck: Wagner, 1892), I, 343, s.n.

7. Cardinal Arnaud d'Ossat (1537-1604), one of the ablest and most successful diplomats of his time. A powerful supporter of Henry IV, in later life he served as his representative in Rome.

8. Pope Clement VIII (1536-1605), reigned from 1592 to 1605. St. Francis de Sales early in life came to his attention and was summoned by him to Rome in 1599. In the presence of various cardinals, including St. Robert Bellar-

NOTES

mine and Caesar Baronius, the Holy Father questioned the young priest, and at the end of the examination said: "Drink my son, from your wellsprings and from your living sources. May these waters issue forth so that everyone may drink his fill from them." Certainly they are words that had more than a little of the prophetic in them.

9. Different as they were in character, St. Francis de Sales and Henry IV had high regard for one another. The king would have liked to keep St. Francis in Paris and wished to see him made a cardinal. There is no truth in the story that Henry IV suggested to St. Francis that he write the *Introduction to the Devout Life*.

10. *Oeuvres* XII, 326-32.

11. Cf. 1 Cor. 12:4-7; "Charity . . . rejoices with the truth . . . believes all things."

12. St. Francis also refers to the subject in a letter to Mme. de Chantal, dated October 14, 1604: "I am writing a letter of five sheets to M. de Bourges where I indicate to him the way to preach, and along with that, I allow myself to give him my advice on several aspects of an archbishop's life." *Oeuvres* XII, 362.

13. "Love equalizes lovers," a Pythagorean maxim.

14. In his introduction to the treatise *On the Love of God*, St. Francis gives an account of how he came to write his various works, including these two books.

15. *Introduction to the Devout Life*. Translated and edited by John K. Ryan, (Garden City, N.Y.: Image Books, Doubleday & Co., Inc., 1959).

16. Declaration of him as blessed on December 28, 1661 by Pope Alexander VII (1599-1667) is generally regarded as the first solemn beatification.

17. Cf. p. 19, n. 2.
18. John 10:10.
19. Cf. pp. 101-02, n. 5.
20. Tim. 4:2.
21. Cf. p. 95, n. 51.
22. An indication of the immensity of his reading is given in Antanas Liuima, *Aux sources du Traité de l'amour de Dieu*. ("Collectanea Spiritualis V and VI." Rome: Librairie Editrice de l'Université Gregorienne, 1959, 1960).

PART ONE: *The Preacher*

1. Cf. Num. 20:8; Ps. 77:16; Is. 48:21.
2. Aristotle's doctrine of the four causes—that by which, that for which, that out of which, and that into which a thing is made, as the efficient, final, material, and formal causes may be briefly described—is found in his *Physics*, Book II, chapter 3, *Posterior Analytics*, Book II, chapter 2, and *Metaphysics*, Book I, chapters 2-6, Book V, chapter 4, and Book XII, chapters 4 and 5, and elsewhere in his works. Cf. *The Basic Works of Aristotle*. Edited by Richard McKeon (New York: Random House, 1941). It is difficult to name another doctrine in philosophy as profound and fruitful as this contribution of Aristotle. As may be seen, St. Francis makes effective use of it in the following pages.
3. As noted in the preface, the subheadings have been inserted by the translator. In the first edition of the letter

similar subheadings were introduced by the editor and they are retained in the Annecy edition. The present subheadings are not translations of those in the Annecy edition.

4. Cf. *Pontificale romanum.* Before his consecration when the bishop is questioned as to his readiness to fulfill his duties, he is asked about teaching the people, first, the Scriptures and, secondly, "the tradition of the orthodox fathers and the decretal constitutions of the Holy and Apostolic See." After he is consecrated he is presented with a book of the gospels with the words: "Receive the gospel and go preach to the people committed to you, for God is powerful to increase his grace in you, he who lives and reigns, world without end. Amen."

5. 1 Cor. 9:16.

6. Cf. H. J. Schroeder, *Canons and Decrees of the Council of Trent.* Original Text with English Translation (St. Louis, Mo.: B. Herder Book Co., 1941), Fifth session, chapter 2, p. 26.

7. St. Francis of Assisi (1181/82-1226), St. Francis de Sales' namesake and patron, was held in veneration by him and is mentioned many times in his writings.

8. St. Charles Borromeo (1538-1584), a cardinal at 22 and archbishop of Milan at 25, one of the greatest names in the counter-reformation and the leading figure in the closing sessions of the council of Trent. Generally recognized as a saint soon after his death, he was canonized in 1610. St. Francis de Sales had great admiration for him and together with some of his clergy made a pilgrimage to his tomb in April, 1613. Will the record of the Second Vatican

council show the presence and influence of someone like St. Charles Borromeo?

9. Desiderius Erasmus (1467-1536). I have not located the reference.

10. St. Francis' variation on "*Faber fit fabricando*: The carpenter is made by carpentering."

11. "In the beginning." John 1:1.

12. "A bishop must be blameless. 1 Tim. 3:2; cf. also Tit. 1:7.

13. "Things that are mere trifles among people in the world are blasphemous acts among the clergy." St. Bernard's words are: "*Inter saeculares nugae, nugae sunt; in ore sacerdotis blasphemiae*: Among people in the world trifles are mere trifles; in a priest's mouth they become blasphemies." *De consideratione*, 1. II, c. xiii, P.L., 182:756. For St. Bernard, Cf. n. 128.

14. St. Francis here refers particularly to "*venatio clamorosa*," hunting with horses and dogs.

15. St. Francis de Sales does not object to buying needed books, and, we may say, he would insist that such books be bought and read by the archbishop. What he rightly condemns is to squander money on a great library of costly books that would fit better into a royal chateau or the mansion of a wealthy layman than into an episcopal residence. His own reading indicates wide use and presumably ownership of needed books, and his statement at the end of the letter about the lack of works on theology and preaching at Sales implies their presence in his house at Annecy. He wishes to stress that for a bishop frugality and simplicity of life are of obligation, and that this holds with

regard to the ownership of books as well as for apparel and at table.

16. "The poor cry out after us: 'What you squander belongs to us; whatever you spend needlessly is cruelly snatched from us.'"

St. Bernard writes: *"Clamant vero nudi, clamant famelici, conqueruntur, et dicunt . . . subtrahitur quod effunditis; nobis crudeliter subtrahitur, quod inaniter expenditis*: The naked cry out, the hungry cry out, they complain, and they say: What you squander is taken away from us; what you spend needlessly is cruelly taken away from us." St. Bernard, *De moribus et officio episcoporum tractatus*, c. II, n. 7, P.L., 182:756.

17. "A bishop must be hospitable." 1 Tim. 3:2. Also Tit. 1:7, 8: "For a bishop must be blameless as being the steward of God, not proud, or ill-tempered, or a drinker, or a brawler, or greedy for base gain; but hospitable, gentle, reserved, just, holy, continent."

18. Cf. Schroeder, *op. cit.*, Twenty-fifth session, Decree concerning Reform, 1, 232, 33.

19. Cf. St. John Chrysostom: "This blood [of Christ] when worthily received drives demons far away, and calls angels and the very Lord of angels to us. Demons flee when they behold the Lord's blood, but angels hasten to it." *Homilia* XLVI *in Ioannem*, n. 3, P.G., 59:261-63.

20. "Do you seek a proof of the Christ who speaks in us?" 2 Cor. 13:3.

21. "As long as I am in the world I am the light of the world." John 9:5.

22. Cf. also John 12:46.

23. Luke 24:31.

24. "But to the wicked man God has said: Why do you recite my statutes, and profess my covenant with your mouth?" Ps. 49:16.

25. "I chastise my body and bring it into subjection, lest perhaps after preaching to others I myself should be rejected." 1 Cor. 9:27.

PART TWO: Light and Warmth

1. "The end is first in intention and last in execution" is a familiar maxim in scholastic philosophy. It is illustrated by St. Thomas Aquinas in *Summa theologica*, 1-2, 1, 1, ad 1. A modern instance may be given. A man determines to repay a debt, and thus this end or final cause originally exists in the intentional order, that is, the order of thought and will, in the man's mind. However, this end, the actual repayment of the debt, does not exist in the order of execution or fact until the debtor has actually delivered his money to the creditor. As St. Francis puts it, the end is the master cause; it in some way dominates the project from its inception to its completion. In *Physics* II, ii, Aristotle writes: "In the arts we prepare the material in view of the end it is to serve, whereas in natural things nature provides the material." In the natural order as in the arts, the material is provided in view of the end that nature has.

2. St. Francis amplifies a scholastic maxim, "*Omne*

NOTES

agens agit propter finem: Every agent acts for some end," which is basic to scholastic teleology. For explanation and uses of the principle, see *Summa theologica*, 1, 19, 4, c; 7, 4, c; 23, 7, c; 47, 3, ad 2; 62, 9, c, and Aristotle, *Physics*, II.

3. "I have come that they may have life, and have it more abundantly." John 10:10.

4. "So that you may root up and destroy . . . and build up and plant." "This day I set you over nations and over kingdoms to root up and to tear down, to destroy and to demolish, to build and to plant." Jer. 1:10.

5. "I have come that these [people here present] may have life and have it more abundantly."

6. The prayer that was long said before recitation of the breviary is recalled: "Open, O Lord, my mouth to bless your holy name; cleanse my heart of all idle, evil, and useless thoughts. Enlighten my understanding and inflame my will, so that I may worthily, attentively, and devoutly recite this office, and merit to be heard with favor in the sight of your divine majesty. Through Christ our Lord. Amen." The writer regrets that this great prayer is no longer obligatory. Cf. John K. Ryan, "A Paradigm for Prayer," *Emmanuel*, October, 1955.

7. Cf. Luke 22:19.

8. Cf. Acts 2:3, "And there appeared to them parted tongues of fire, which settled upon each of them."

9. Cf. St. Bernard, *Sermo* II *in festo Pentecostes*, nn. 7, 8, P.L., 183: 329, 30.

10. Cf. 1 Cor. 1:23; 2:2.

11. "We do not seek after the rhetoricians' charms but

the truths of the fishermen." This thought is developed by St. Ambrose: "Christian preaching does not need showy, elegant discourse, and therefore fishermen, uneducated men, were chosen to spread the Gospel." *Commentaria in epistolam primam ad Corinthios*, P.L., 17:188. The Comment is on 1 Cor. 1:17. Also by St. Augustine: "If he [Christ] had first chosen an orator, that orator would say, 'My eloquence has been chosen,' . . . A fisherman puts away his nets, a sinner accepts grace, and is made a divine orator. Hence now the words of fishermen are read, and the necks of the orators are bowed down." *Sermo* LXXXVII, c. x, P.L., 38:537.

12. "Itching ears." Cf. "For there will come a time when they will not endure the sound doctrine; but having itching ears, will heap up to themselves teachers according to their hearts." 2 Tim. 4:3.

13. See note 3.

PART THREE: *The Word of God*

1. "Preach the word." Cf. "I charge thee in the sight of God and Christ Jesus . . . preach the word, be urgent in season, out of season." 2 Tim. 4:2.

2. "Preach the gospel." Cf. "And he said to them, 'Go into the whole world and preach the gospel to every creature.'" Mark 16:15.

3. *Regula secunda*, c. ix, in *Gli scritti di san Francesco*

NOTES

d'Assisi e "I fioretti," a cura di Augusto Vincinelli (Milan: Arnoldo Mondadori, 1955), p. 121.

4. Cf. St. Jerome, *Epistola* LXVI, *ad Pammachium*, n. 8, P.L., 22:644.

5. Cf. Deut. 21:11-13.

6. "To separate the precious from the vile." Cf. "If you bring forth the precious without the vile, you shall be my mouthpieces." Jer. 15:19.

7. Cf. introduction, p. 15 for St. Francis' use of Plutarch.

8. In addition to countless passages from the Greek and Roman philosophers—not only Aristotle, Plato, Plotinus, Porphyry, Macrobius, Cicero, Seneca, Heraclitus, and many others—quoted by a medieval scholastic like St. Thomas Aquinas, it is necessary to point out that he quotes various poets, for instance, Horace, Terence, and Aristophanes. It may also be noted that quotations from the pagan poets and others found their way into the liturgy. Examples are Vergil's *"non talibus auxiliis,"* (not by such aids) (*Aeneid*, II, 521.2), which appears at least twice, and Seneca's *"philosophiae servire libertas est"*: "to serve philosophy is freedom," adapted in the postcommunion prayer in the Mass for peace and elsewhere: *"Deus ... cui servire regnare est*: "God ... whom to serve is to reign."

9. "For in him we live and move and have our being, as indeed some of your own poets have said, 'For we are also his offspring.'" The line quoted by St. Paul is by Aratus of Soli (c. 315-240/239 B.C.), the Stoic poet, a native of Cilicia, as was St. Paul. Cf. his astronomical poem

entitled *Phaenomena*, I, 2-5: "Full of gods are all the streets and all the marketplaces of men. Full is the sea, and the heavens thereof. Always we have need of God, for we are also his offspring."

10. "One of themselves, a prophet of their own, said, 'Cretans, always liars; evil beasts, lazy, gluttons.' This statement is true." Tit. 1:12. The words quoted, at least the first part, are by Epimenides of Gnossus in Crete, a religious teacher of the late sixth and early fifth centuries B.C., sometimes named as one of the Seven Sages. He is mentioned by Plato (*Laws*, I, 642 d). According to St. Jerome, the quotation is from Epimenides' oracles. Cf. Kathleen Freeman, *Ancilla to the Pre-Socratic Philosophers* (Cambridge, Mass.: Harvard University Press, 1948), pp. 9-11. St. Paul does not quote Menander (c. 343-291 B.C.), the great comic dramatist.

11. Cf. St. Ambrose, *In psalmum* XLIII *enarratio*, n. 73. P.L., 14:1124, where he likens pagan literature to the sirens' songs.

12. Cf. 1 Kings 5:2.

13. St. Francis de Sales' own works are filled with analogies and illustrations taken from nature or from books by natural historians, especially Pliny. *On the Love of God* contains 43 uses of Pliny and the *Introduction to the Devout Life* has 29. Aristotle is also a source of such material. St. Francis is fond of illustrations and analogies taken from country life in Savoy.

14. The mystical or symbolic interpretation of the universe as a book written by God to be read by those

knowing its language had ancient origins but reached its most elaborate, and in some cases its most extravagant, development in the Middle Ages. The Victorine school of mystics—so named from the Augustinian abbey of St. Victor in Paris—had this as one of its chief doctrines. Its greatest representative is Hugh of St. Victor (1096-1141). Cf. P. Pourrat, *Christian Spirituality in the Middle Ages*. Tr. S. P. Jacques (New York: P. J. Kenedy and Sons, 1924), pp. 100-132. Etienne Gilson, *History of Christian Philosophy in the Middle Ages* (New York: Random House, 1955), pp. 164-171; 630-35.

15. Cf. St. Athanasius, *The Life of Saint Anthony*. Newly translated and annotated by Robert T. Meyer ("Ancient Christian Writers, No. 14," Westminster, Md.: The Newman Press, 1950), p. 21. In his *Confessions* St. Augustine tells of his first acquaintance with St. Athanasius' biography of St. Anthony and of the effect it had on certain others. Cf. *The Confessions of St. Augustine*. Translated, with an introduction and notes by John K. Ryan (Garden City, N. Y.: Image Books, 1960), pp. 190-93.

16. "God's invisible attributes are clearly seen . . . being understood through the things that are made." Cf. Rom. 1:19, 20.

17. "The heavens proclaim the glory of God." Ps. 18:1. The line may be taken as a succinct statement of the teleological argument for God's existence.

18. "From the lesser to the greater," as in Luke 23:31: "For if in the green wood they do these things, what is to happen in the case of the dry?"

19. "Go to the ant." Prov. 6:6.
20. "As the hen gathers her young." Matt. 23:37.
21. "As the hind longs for . . ." Ps. 41:1.
22. "Like the ostrich in the desert." Lam. 4:3.
23. "Consider the lilies of the field." Matt. 6:28.

24. Undoubtedly St. Francis de Sales had reason to give the warnings contained in this passage. Periodic scares over witchcraft, supposed demoniac possession, asserted visions and miracles, and the like provided material for lurid writers and preachers in Catholic countries as well as elsewhere, for instance, in seventeenth-century England and New England. The warnings are not unneeded at the present time, but the modern aberration is not so much to preach on such subjects as on topics of the day and current trivialities rather than on the gospel. Worse still it is not to preach at all. If we were forbidden by the state to preach the gospel, we would rightly consider it a gross form of censorship and religious persecution. If we do not preach, we bring about the same result. Self-silencing can be more effective and pernicious than silence imposed by a persecutor.

25. The argument from God's authority as evidenced in Scripture is paramount in theology. As St. Thomas Aquinas puts it in *Summa theologica*, 1, 1, 8, ad 3:

> Arguments from authority are in an especial way proper to this doctrine, inasmuch as its principles are obtained from revelation. Hence we ought to believe on the authority of those to whom the revelation has been made. Nor does this take away from the dignity

NOTES

of this doctrine, for although the argument from authority based on human reason is the weakest, the argument from authority based on divine revelation is the most effective. Sacred doctrine also makes use of human reason, not indeed to prove faith—for thereby the merit of faith would come to an end—but to make clear certain other things that are put forward in this doctrine. Therefore, since grace does not destroy nature but perfects it, natural reason should minister to faith as the natural inclination of the will ministers to charity.

26. "He himself has said it," the αὐτὸς ἔφα of the Pythagoreans when quoting Pythagoras and of the Epicureans when quoting Epicurus.

27. "The master has said these things."

28. "My teaching is not my own, but his who sent me." John 7:16.

29. "The letter teaches facts; allegory what you must believe; anagogy what you should hope for; tropology what you must do." St. Thomas Aquinas discusses the four senses of Scripture in various places. In *Summa theologica*, 1, 1, 10, which is entitled, "Whether Sacred Scripture has many meanings under one word," he writes:

The author of Sacred Scripture is God, who has the power to accommodate words to express not only meanings, which man too can do, but likewise things themselves. Therefore, since in all sciences words have meaning, this science has the property that the very things signified by words also signify something. Hence, that primary signification, whereby the words signified things, pertains to the first sense, which is the historical or literal sense. That signification whereby the things signified by the words in turn signify other things is called the spiritual sense. It is based on the literal sense and supposes it. This spiritual sense is divided in three ways. As the apostle says (Hebrews 7), the Old Law is a figure of the New Law, and, as Dionysius says in his *Ecclesiastical Hierarchy*, ch. 5, part 1, "it is a figure of future glory." In the New Law things done in its head are signs of things we ought to do. Hence in so far as the things of the Old Law signify the things of the New Law there is an allegorical sense. In so far as the things done in Christ, or done in things that signify Christ, are signs of what we ought to do, there is the moral sense. In so far as they signify things that are in eternal glory, there is the anagogical sense. Since the literal sense is what the author intends, and since the author of Sacred Scripture is God, who simultaneously comprehends all things by his intellect, it is not unfitting, as Augustine says (*Confessions*, Book 12, ch. 18-20, 24, and 31) 'if in keeping with the literal sense in a single scriptural word there may be many meanings.' "

Cf. C. Spicq, *Esquisse d'une histoire de l'exégèse latine au moyen âge* (Paris: J. Vrin, 1944) and H. de Lubac, "Sur un vieux distique; la doctrine du 'quadruple sens,' " *Mélanges offerts au R. P. Ferdinand Cavalerra* (Toulouse: Bibliothèque de l'Institut catholique, 1948) pp. 347-66.

30. Thorens, Savoy, where St. Francis preached on October 3, 1604, the seventeenth Sunday after Pentecost, on the gospel of the Sunday, Matt. 22:35-46. Since this letter is so lengthy and is dated "October 5," it is likely that

St. Francis worked on it for more than one day. He had previously referred to October 4, the feast of St. Francis of Assisi, as "yesterday." Hence, this reference to Sunday, October 3, as yesterday is a slip of the pen, or perhaps an indication that he worked on this section before some of the earlier parts. His letter to President Frémyot, dated October 7, states that he is sending a letter to the archbishop, and an even longer letter to Mme. de Chantal, dated October 14, says that he is writing it.

31. "Thou shalt love the Lord thy God with thy whole heart, thy whole soul, thy whole mind." Cf. Deut. 6:5; Matt. 22:37.

32. St. Bernard, *Sermo XX in Cantica*, n. 6. P.L., 183:869-70.

33. "According to knowledge and discretion." Cf. Rom. 10:2.

34. "*Diligere*: to love" and "*eligo*: I choose." Cf. St. Thomas Aquinas, *Summa theologica*, 1-2, 26, 3.

35. Cf. Rom. 6:19.

36. "So that the gentiles may know that they are but men." Ps. 9:21.

37. "Say that we are unprofitable servants." Cf. Luke 17:10.

38. "It is not mine to give you." Matt. 20:23.

39. The reference is to an outline for a sermon to be preached on March 17, 1604, the Wednesday after the second Sunday in Lent. St. Francis' memory was not at fault, as he does not refer to St. Hilary's interpretation. The notes indicate that he planned to use material drawn

from Pliny, Tacitus, Aelian, and Diogenes Laertius as well as from Scripture, the Fathers of the Church, and other sources. Cf. *Oeuvres*, VIII, 9, 10.

40. Cf. Rom. 9:11-13.

41. Cf. Gal. 4:25, 26.

42. Heb. 12:22, 23.

43. Cf. 3 Kings 19:4, 5.

44. "When two men are fighting and the wife of one intervenes to save her husband from the blows of his opponent, if she stretches forth her hand and seizes the latter by his private parts, you shall chop off her hand without pity." Deut. 25:11, 12.

45. "Two nations are in your womb, and two peoples shall stem from your womb. One people shall be stronger than the other, and the elder shall serve the younger." Gen. 25:23.

46. Cf. Gen. 2:7; 1 Cor. 15:45, 46.

47. "He who made you without you will not save you without you." Cf. St. Augustine, *Sermo* CLXIX, c. xi, P.L., 38:923, where *"justificat"* (justifies) is found instead of St. Francis' *"salvabit."*

48. "He who has promised pardon to those who do penance has not promised a time to do penance." Cf. St. Augustine, *Enarratio in psalmum* CI, *Sermo* I, n. 10, P.L., 37:1301: *"Indulgentiam tibi Deus promisit; crastinum diem tibi nemo promisit*: God has promised forgiveness to you, but no one has promised you a tomorrow." That is, no one should put off doing penance for his sins, because he does not know the day or the hour of his death.

NOTES

49. The reference is to the index to all the works of St. Thomas Aquinas made by Peter of Bergamo, an Italian Dominican who died at Piacenza in 1482. His complete index, made up of two earlier works, was published at Venice in 1497 and at Rome in 1535. Included in the edition of the *opera omnia* of St. Thomas Aquinas published by order of St. Pius V in 1570 (the *editio piana*) under the title *Tabula aurea eximii doctoris Fr. Petri de Bergamo . . . in omnes libros, opuscula, et commentarii D. Thomae Aquinatis*, it has since become known as the "*tabula aurea*" or golden table.

50. Cf. Gen. 22. St. Francis has a beautiful analysis of the sacrifice of Isaac by Abraham in *On the Love of God*, Book 12, chapter 10.

51. Cf. p. 13. The practice has reached its lowest depths in some of the fictionalized biographies and historical novels of our own time. St. Francis' criticism illustrates his sense of historical accuracy, insistence on correct doctrine, and good taste in preaching and writing as well as elsewhere.

52. Cf. Luke 15:4-7.

53. Cf. Matt. 13:3-23.

54. Cf. Ps. 102:5.

55. "Their memory has perished with a noise." Cf. Ps. 9:7 in the Douay Version.

56. 1 Cor. 13:1.

57. "I have run ("*cucurri*") the way of thy commandments, when thou didst enlarge ("*dilatasti*") my heart." Cf. Ps. 118:32.

58. Cf. St. Bonaventure's *Life of St. Francis*, chapter 7, translated by E. Gurney Salter, in *The Little Flowers of St. Francis, the Mirror of Perfection, The Life of St. Francis* (New York: E. P. Dutton, 1947), p. 347. Bonaventure was the second name of St. Francis de Sales and he had a special devotion to the great Franciscan thinker.

59. "The bread of angels."

60. "Man ate the bread of angels." Cf. Ps. 77:25, in the Douay Version.

61. "Everyone who exalts himself shall be humbled." Luke 14:11.

62. By "an entire gospel" St. Francis means the whole gospel of the Mass of the day when the sermon is preached.

63. St. Francis does this in a sermon preached on April 12, 1594, the Tuesday of Easter week, on the text "Peace to you" (Luke 24:36; John 20:19-21). Cf. *Oeuvres*, VII, Sermon XVII.

64. Cf. 1 Cor. 6:14; 2 Cor. 4:14.

65. Cf. Acts 1:3-6.

66. See pp. 58-59, n. 77.

67. "How didst thou come in here without a wedding garment?" Matt. 22:12.

68. Bernardino Rossignolo (1563-1613), an Italian Jesuit, author of *De actionibus virtutis, ex s. scripturis et patribus libri duo* (Venice, 1603).

69. The reference is to the great funeral sermon preached over Prince Philip Emmanuel of Lorraine, Duke of Mercoeur, delivered in Notre Dame cathedral in Paris, on April 27, 1602, at the request of the duke's widow,

NOTES

Marie of Luxembourg. St. Francis also refers to the sermon in his introduction to his theatise *On the Love of God*, I, 46, 47. It is the only sermon that he published. The text is given in *Oeuvres*, VII, 400-35.

70. "That one may live piously towards God, temperately towards oneself, justly towards one's neighbor." St. Francis' words are an adaptation of Tit. 2:12.

71. "By acting."

72. "By suffering."

73. "By praying."

74. "All that is in the world is the lust of the flesh, etc." 1 John 2:16.

75. Fontaines-les-Dijon is the birthplace of St. Bernard.

76. "Humility," "humble," "pride," and "proud."

77. "Feigned humility," "indiscreet humility."

78. "For an intelligent man a few words are enough," a variation of "*Verbum sapienti satis*: A word to the wise is sufficient."

79. Among the works of St. Thomas that St. Francis uses in his most important book, the treatise *On the Love of God*, are *Summa theologica*, *Scriptum super IV libros Sententiarum magistri Petri Lombardi*, *Quaestiones disputatae De malo*, *De ente et essentia*, *Commentaria in Aristotelis Physica*, and *in X libros Ethicorum Aristotelis*. He undoubtedly made use of such other works as the *Summa contra gentiles*, the scriptural commentaries, and various *opuscula*.

80. St. Antoninus (1389-1459), archbishop of Florence, Dominican, author of *Summa theologiae moralis* (Venice,

1477-80), *Summula confessorum* (Mainz, 1460), Rome, 1472; Venice, 1480), *Juris pontificii et caesarei summa* (Venice, 1582).

81. Gulielmus Peraldus (Peraltuse, Perault, de Petra alta, etc.), a thirteenth-century Dominican, also known as Lugdunensis because he was for ten years coadjutor bishop of Lyons under Philip of Savoy, who occupied the see from 1246 to 1267. He was the author of *Summa aurea de virtutibus et vitiis* (Cologne, 1479).

82. Philip Diez, a sixteenth-century Spanish Franciscan (+1601), author of *Conciones quaruplices in Evangelia* (Salamanca, 1682).

83. Hieronymus Orosius (1506-1580), bishop of Sylves, a Portuguese Dominican, author of *Paraphrases et commentarii in s. scripturam* (Rome, 1592).

84. Louis of Granada (1555-1588), Spanish Dominican theologian, author of many works, including *La guia de pecadores* (Badajoz, 1555; Salamanca, 1570), of which there was an early French translation by Paul du Mont, *La guide des pecheurs* (Douay, 1574); later by Nicholas Colin (Rheims, 1577), and *Memorial de la vida christiana*, first of six parts translated into French by G. de Pilly (Paris, 1575); second by N. Colin, *Memorial de la vie chretienne* (Rheims, 1577). In a letter to M. Antoine de Revol, bishop elect of Dol, St. Francis names these books and recommends Granada's works in the highest terms: "*Ayés, je vous prie, Grenade tout entier, et que ce soit vostre second breviaire.*" *Oeuvres*, XII, 189. Among Louis of Granada's works translated in whole or in part into English are:

Summa of the Christian Life. Selected texts . . . translated and adopted by Jordan Aumann, 3 vols. (St. Louis: B. Herder, 1954, 1955); *The Sinner's Guide* (Philadelphia: Kilner, 1883), and *Memorial of a Christian Life* (New York: McSorley, 1868), both translated anonymously.

85. Maurice Hylaret (1539-1591), Franciscan, author of *Sacrae decades quinquepartitae: Conciones quadragesimales atque paschales* (Lyons, 1591), *Sermons catholiques*, and other works.

86. Diego Stella (1524-1595), Spanish Franciscan, author of *Commentarii in Lucae evangelium* (Alcala, 1578). In his letter to Bishop de Revol St. Francis recommends Stella's work on the vanity of the world, which had been translated into Italian as *Il dispreggio della vanità del mondo* (Venice, 1575). Cf. *Oeuvres*, XII, 190.

87. Alfonso Salmeron (1515-1595), a Spaniard, author of *Commentarii in evangelicam historiam et in Acta apostolorum* (Madrid, 1598-1602).

88. Sebastian Barradas (1543-1615), Portuguese, author of *Commentarii in concordiam et historiam evangelicam* (Coimbra, 1599). Hurter quotes Cornelius à Lapide as praising Barradas for his interpretation of the moral content of Scripture.

89. St. Gregory I (c. 538-604), the Great, pope and doctor of the Church, author of *Moralia, Dialogues*, and *Regula Pastoralis*. Cf. *Pastoral Care*, tr. and ed. Henry Davis (Westminster, Md.: The Newman Press, 1950).

90. St. John Chrysostom (c. 344-354-407), patriarch of Constantinople, called Chrysostom—Golden Mouth—

because of his eloquence, one of the greatest of the Greek fathers and doctors. St. Francis doubtless refers especially to his scriptural homilies. Cf. Johannes Quasten, *Patrology*, Vol. III (Westminster, Md.: The Newman Press, 1960), pp. 424-82.

91. St. Bernard (1091-1153), abbot of Clairvaux, canonized in 1174 and named doctor of the Church in 1830. Because of his Burgundian birth in Fontaines castle near Dijon, St. Francis refers to him as "our doctor."

92. Hieronymus Lauretus, a sixteenth-century Benedictine of Montserrat, later abbot of Guixoles, author of *Sylva allegoriarum totius s. Scripturae* (Paris, 1584).

93. Jean Benedicti (1484-1573), a Sorbonne doctor, author of *Scholia in universam s. Scripturam* (Paris, 1541).

PART FOUR: *How We Must Preach*

1. Aristotle has various statements equivalent to this dictum, for instance, "The form is nature." Cf. *Physics*, Book 2. The statement quoted by St. Francis is from a medieval compilation called *Sententiae ex Aristotele*.

2. Among other things this passage reflects the Stoic influence on St. Francis in matters of style as well as otherwise. The Stoic norms of good writing are reported by Diogenes Laertius, whose lives of the Greek philosophers were familiar to St. Francis and used by him in the treatise *On the Love of God* and elsewhere. Diogenes Laeritius writes: "There are five excellences of speech—pure Greek,

lucidity, conciseness, appropriateness, distinction. By good Greek is meant language faultless in point of grammar and free from careless vulgarity. Lucidity is a style which presents the thought in a way easily understood; conciseness a style that employs no more words than are necessary for setting forth the subject in hand; appropriateness lies in a style akin to the subject; distinction is the avoidance of colloquialism." Cf. *Lives of Eminent Philosophers.* With an English translation by R. D. Hicks. 2 vols. (Cambridge, Mass.: Harvard University Press, 1950), "The Life of Zeno," VII, 59, Vol. 2, pp. 169-71. St. Francis' style meets each of these five requirements, including that of economy. If he writes at length, it is not because he uses unneeded words but because he has much to say.

3. *Rhetoricae ecclesiasticae, sive de ratione concionandi libri VI* (Lisbon, 1576), VI, xiii. Cf. J. Quétif and J. Echard, *Scriptores ordinis Praedicatorum* (Paris: 1719-1723), II, pars 1, p. 287.

4. Apparently the bell was rung to indicate to the preacher that it was time for him to stop, perhaps for some special service, for instance, the Angelus. At any rate, St. Francis was rightly annoyed when it was rung too soon, and the quick temper that he had brought under control by years of self-discipline flared up. He admits his fault, but with characteristic honesty, and perhaps out of a sense of duty, adds that he does not like frivolity and undue familiarity. Buffoonery in church must have been especially bad in his eyes.

5. This definition sums up the essential character of

preaching as St. Francis de Sales sees it. It is not merely a personally verbal definition that he gives, that is, merely a statement of how he uses the term. It is rather a socially verbal definition, a statement of what preaching is according to Catholic theology. But it is much more than a verbal definition, a statement of what St. Francis de Sales and other scientific theologians mean by the word preaching. It is a real definition, a statement of the essence of the thing in question. It gives the essential, objective nature of preaching in terms of its four causes. The material cause is God's will; the formal cause its public declaration; the efficient cause, one sent to preach. It will be noted that the definition gives both the proximate and the remote final cause of preaching, the latter being the salvation of the hearer.

All real definitions are causal definitions in so far as they give one or more of the four causes. However, causal definitions that state all four causes, as does this one of preaching, are rare. The definition of a sacrament as an outward sign, instituted by Christ, to give grace, is an example of a causal definition which includes not only efficient and final causes but also the material and formal causes. The traditional definition of law is another example of a definition in which all four causes are found.

PART FIVE: *A Personal Appeal*

1. Cardinal Borromeo had a slight impediment in his speech.

NOTES

2. "Feed my sheep." "Dost thou love me?" Cf. John 20:15-17.

3. Cf. St. Jerome, *Commentaria in epistolam ad Galatas,* II, 15; P.L., 26:433.

4. Archbishop Frémyot's predecessor at Bourges was Renaud de Beaune (1527-1606), bishop of Mende (1568-1581), archbishop of Bourges (1581-1603), and archbishop of Sens (1602-1606). Pope Clement VIII refused for several years to ratify his nomination to Sens. He was renowned for his eloquence and for his devotion to King Henry IV.

5. Cf. Introduction, p. 6.

6. 2 Cor. 5:19.

Bibliography

BIBLIOGRAPHY

De Sales, St. Francis. *Introduction to the Devout Life*.
Translated and edited by John K. Ryan. New York:
Harper and Brothers, 1950; Garden City, New York:
Image Books, 1959.

————. *Les epistres du bien-heureux Messire François de
Sales, evesque et prince de Genève, instituteur de
l'ordre de la Visitation de saincte Marie*. Diviseés en
sept livres . . . Recuellies par Messire Louys de Sales,
prevost de l'eglise de Genève. A Lyon, par Vincent
de Coeursilly . . . M. D.C. XXVI.

————. *Oeuvres de Saint François de Sales, evêque et
prince de Genève et docteur de l'église. Édition com-
plète d'après les autographes et les éditions originales
enrichie de nombreuses pièces inédites* . . . publiée par
les soins des Religieuses de la Visitation du Ier Monas-
tere d'Annecy. 26 vols. Annecy: 1892-1932.

————. *On the Love of God*. Translated and with an Introduction and Notes by John K. Ryan. Garden City,
N.Y.: Image Books, 1963.

————. *Selected Letters*. Translated with an Introduction
by Elisabeth Stopp. London: Faber and Faber, 1960.

Burton, Harold. *The Life of St. Francis de Sales*. 2 vols.
New York: P.J. Kenedy and Sons, 1926, 1929.

ON THE PREACHER AND PREACHING

Camus, Jean Pierre. *The Spirit of Saint François de Sales.* Translated by C. F. Kelley. New York: Harper and Brothers, 1952.

Hamon, André. *Vie de Saint François de Sales.* Nouvelle édition entièrement. Revisée par J. F. Gonthier et G. Letourneau. 2 vols. Paris: Gabalda, 1922.

INDEX

Abraham, 44, 48, 49, 95
Adam, 46
Aelian, 15, 94
Alexander the Great, 15, 38
Alexander VII, Pope, 11, 79
Ambrose, St., 15, 39, 86, 88
Anthony of Egypt, St., 15, 39, 89
Antoninus of Florence, St., 15, 59, 97
Aratus, 15, 39, 87
Aristophanes, 87
Aristotle, 12, 15, 77, 80, 87, 88, 100
Athanasius, St., 15, 89
Augustine, St., 15, 47, 86, 94, 99

Barradas, Sebastian, 15, 59, 99
Baronius, Caesar, 79
Beaune, Renaud de, 103
Bellarmine, St. Robert, 78
Benedicti, Jean, 60, 100
Bernard, St., 15, 25, 26, 39, 41, 47, 49, 57, 59, 82, 83, 97, 100
Bonaventure, St., 15, 96

Caesar, Julius, 15 ,38
Charles Borromeo, St., 15, 16, 24, 81, 82, 100
Cicero, 77, 87

Clement VIII, Pope, 6, 11, 78, 103
Cornelius à Lapide, 99
Coulanges, Marie de, 78

Dagon, 39
David, 27, 50
Diez, Philip, 15, 59, 98
Diogenes Laertius, 94, 100

Elias, 43, 44
Epimenides, 88
Epicurus, 91
Erasmus, Desiderius, 15, 24, 82
Esau, 43-46

Francis de Sales, St., vii, viii, 3-17, 74, 77-103
Francis of Assisi, St., 24, 37, 52, 81, 86, 93, 96
Frémyot, André, 4-9, 11, 17, 77, 79, 103
    Bénigne, 5, 7, 8, 77, 93

God, 9-12, 16, 21, 32, 33, 37-39, 42, 45, 46, 48, 53, 54, 57, 66, 67, 72, 64, 81, 83-86, 88-94, 97, 102
Granier, Claude de, 11
Gregory the Great, St., 15, 59, 99